Should
I Kiss
or
Shake Hands?

2006-7 NMI
MISSION EDUCATION RESOURCES

✳ ✳ ✳

BOOKS

EIGHT STEPS FROM THE EDGE OF HELL
From Addiction to Ministry in Ukraine
by Sherry Pinson

EVERY FULL-MOON NIGHT
Life Lessons from Missionary Kids
by Dean Nelson

GLIMPSES OF GRACE
Mission Stories from Bolivia
by Randy Bynum

THE POWER OF ONE
Compassion as a Lifestyle
by Ellen Decker

SHOULD I KISS OR SHAKE HANDS?
Surviving in Another Culture
by Pat Stockett Johnston

SHOUTS AT SUNRISE
The Abduction and Rescue of Don Cox
by Keith Schwanz

✳ ✳ ✳

ADULT MISSION EDUCATION RESOURCE BOOK

MISSION FAMILIES
Editors: Wes Eby and Rosanne Bolerjack

Should
I Kiss
or
Shake Hands?

Surviving in Another Culture

by
Pat Stockett Johnston

Nazarene Publishing House
Kansas City, Missouri

Copyright 2006
by Nazarene Publishing House

ISBN 083-412-2367

Printed in the United States of America

Editor: Wes Eby
Cover Design: Chad Cherry

10   9   8   7   6   5   4   3   2   1

Dedication

I dedicate this book to four special people.

- Only one was born when her parents responded to God's call to missions.
- None grew up in their own home country.
- English, their mother tongue, was not the mother tongue of their neighbors.
- All sang in Arabic, Armenian, French, Turkish, and Pidgin English, as well as English.
- From birth to 18 they attended school, went to church on Sunday, took piano lessons, played Little League baseball, joined Brownies and Cub Scouts, cared for pets, learned to swim, made friends—mostly in countries of which they were not citizens.
- Their toughest cultural adjustments happened during furloughs in the United States.
- They never complained about their parents' strange call that separated them from family and country.
- They're best described as supportive, cooperative, caring, flexible, resilient. Survivors all.

Thank you, Beverly, Keith, Joanne, and Craig.

Love,
Mom

Contents

Pat Stockett Johnston and her husband, Gordon, served for 34 years as global missionaries for the Church of the Nazarene in Lebanon, Jordan, and Papua New Guinea. They now reside in Temple City, California. An ordained minister, Pat is a speaker at women's retreats, conferences, and missions events.

Pat grew up in a Nazarene parsonage. After graduation from Pasadena College (now Point Loma Nazarene University), she became a pastor's wife, earned a master's degree from California State University, and taught for six years in public schools.

As a freelance writer, Pat has had articles published in *The Other Sheep* and *World Mission, Herald of Holiness* and *Holiness Today,* and *Come Ye Apart.* Pat has authored four books for the NMI (Nazarene Missions International) educational program: *Journey to Jerusalem: Making a Difference in the Middle East; Is That You, God?: Responses to the Missions Call; Changed Hearts, Changed Lives;* and *City of Fear* (for older children).

The Johnstons have four children—Beverly Hines, Keith, Joanne Davies, and Craig—and five grandchildren.

Foreword

"If I have seen further it is by standing on the shoulders of giants." So states Sir Isaac Newton in the *Oxford Dictionary of Quotations.*

Reflecting on the more than 25 years of missionary service for my family and me, I realize how important our few years of living in another land were. Pat Stockett Johnston and her husband, Gordon, were with us when we first flew into Amman, Jordan. We also had the opportunity to be with them at their retirement when they said good-bye to the people they had loved and served.

As they stood tall all the way, we were able to learn from them and see down the road a bit further while standing on their shoulders of experience and faithfulness. Few missionaries have faced the challenges they dealt with for 34 years: the Lebanese civil war, emergency evacuation, family illness (five of the six Johnstons had hepatitis at the same time), separation from children sent to boarding school, and tribal wars in Papua New Guinea, just to name a few. They remained positive, caring, loving, and tenacious to their ever-present missionary call—a call they neither doubted nor regretted—and that taught Kay and me that we could do it too.

From this tenacity and an amazing sense of humor, Pat writes from firsthand experience. As we have personally done with her many times, you will laugh with her and cry with her. You will rejoice in

God's faithfulness in how He helps the ones He calls to overcome their own cultural biases to work more effectively with the people of other lands—and to bless and be blessed by them. The Johnstons are true survivors.

Lindell R. Browning
Eastern Mediterranean Field director

Acknowledgments

I could not have written this book without valuable contributions from the following missionaries, current and retired:

Larry Buess—Lebanon and Jordan
Lindell Browning, Eastern Mediterranean Field director
Charles Gates—Brazil
Carolyn Parson Hannay—Haiti and Papua New Guinea
Al and Kitty Jones—Kenya, Ethiopia, and Australia
Ivan Lathrop—Jordan, Lebanon, Germany, and Japan
Norma Weis Morgan—India and Israel
Mary Mercer—Korea
Maryel Moyer—Republic of South Africa and Kenya
Warren Neal—Papua New Guinea and East Timor
Donald Owens, general superintendent emeritus, Church
    of the Nazarene—Korea
Connie Patrick—Albania, Papua New Guinea, and
    Switzerland
Phyllis Perkins, former general NMI director—Japan
Harold Ray—Guatemala and Argentina
Philip Rodebush—Bulgaria, Jordan, and Israel
Elizabeth Sedat—Guatemala
Henry (Harry) and Grace Stevenson—Mexico, Bolivia,
    Spain, Ireland, Israel, and Jordan
Judy Slater Webb—Republic of South Africa and Bolivia
Larry Webb—Barbados, Mexico, and Bolivia

Thank you, one and all,
Pat Stockett Johnston

Introduction

"Diane, how did it go?"

I could hardly wait for my friend's response, for she had just returned to the United States from an overseas Work and Witness trip.

"Well," she grimaced, "it wasn't what I imagined."

"And why was that?" I asked.

"I anticipated at least enough water for daily showers and washing clothes—and safe drinking water from the faucet. In my bedroom the little space heater barely cut the chill. When traveling, I sometimes had to close my eyes to avoid seeing how close other vehicles drove to our bus. And I missed sliced bread. No stores sold Dr. Pepper—my favorite soft drink. Our accommodations didn't even have a television, much less cable TV. And since I didn't speak the local language, I felt like a foreigner. Pat, I was way out of my comfort zone!"

It was obvious that Diane's experience in another land fell far short of her expectations. The same was true for my son-in-law Rick's first visit to the United States from England.

"I was stressed from the moment I walked into the 'arrivals' section of the airport," Rick said. "No trolleys (baggage cars) were in sight, and when I finally spotted a line of carts, a sign said I had to pay to use one. That demanded I first visit the *bureau de change* for U.S. money. Then I was told to stand in line for customs. I looked all over for a line on the floor, only to find out that Americans don't queue, they line up.

"Plenty of yellow cars stood outside the departure door. 'Taxi,' not 'cab,' was written on their lighted signs. As I approached a taxi driver, he asked, 'Do you want to put your luggage in the trunk?'

"*What trunk?* I wondered. *Why would a suitcase need to go into a trunk?* I finally worked out that the driver meant 'boot.'

"The motorway to the hotel was frightening—eight lines on each side at one section. It made England's M5 look like a country lane.

"My room was *en suite,* so I headed for the shower. But where were the hot and cold water taps? How was I to control the water temperature? One odd-looking fixture was attached under the showerhead. I determined this push-me, pull-me, twist-me, turn-me contraption needed to come with directions.

"Skimpy meals all day made me really hungry for breakfast the next morning. I was going to order a full English breakfast, I decided. Poached eggs on toast, blood sausage and bacon, accompanied by a grilled tomato, fried mushrooms, and a cup of hot tea. Was I in for a shock!

"'Sir, we don't serve poached eggs,' the waiter said. 'You can have your eggs scrambled hard or soft, or fried sunny-side up, over easy, over medium, or over hard. Hard-boiled eggs will cost you extra. And our sausage is Jimmy Dean. Will that do?'

"By now my brain was scrambled. The worst

14

was yet to come in form of a stainless-steel pot filled with lukewarm water; a tea bag stood propped against the saucer. 'Don't Americans know tea needs to be made from water just off a rolling boil?' I fumed to myself. My tea was undrinkable. Unfortunately, the only drink left was a glass of water—with ice in it! *It's my first meal in America*, I thought, *and I already want to go back home."*

Diane and Rick both discovered that going to another country generates cultural stress; that other countries rarely mirror "home" in every detail of life. No one is immune to cultural stress. Adjustment difficulties will be encountered, and a range of lifestyle changes will be necessary to feel comfortable in another land and culture.

The six chapters in *Do I Kiss or Shake Hands?* are arranged in the order in which adjustment issues often occur. The first chapter begins with immediately needed information about safe drinking water. Other chapters describe differences in food and diet, driving patterns, language learning, and culture. The last chapter discusses how religion shapes culture.

Committed Nazarenes are increasingly becoming involved in ministries outside their home countries. Success in their endeavors demands adjustments to different cultures. Reading (or listening to) this book will not save travelers from cultural stress, but it will give them valuable clues that can help in making a new and different land feel like home.

1 Is This Safe to Drink?

My husband, Gordon, and I never dreamed that water would be an issue when we made our first overseas move. We presumed that everybody everywhere had drinkable (potable) water available in their homes via faucets 24 hours a day, 7 days a week. It didn't take us long to understand that the most important question to ask in a new place was "Where can we find drinkable water?"

We became aware of this important question in 1969 on the first day of our first trans-Atlantic journey. Our itinerary from Los Angeles to Beirut included a one-night layover in Paris. Air France put us up in a quaint hotel in downtown Paris. The ticket voucher included the evening meal. We had never eaten in a French restaurant before and had quite a giggle at the stack of plates surrounded by an overwhelming amount of knives, forks, and spoons at each place setting. But our biggest surprise came when the waiter presented us with the bottle of wine that accompanied the evening meal.

"We would just like some water, please," Gordon said.

With a bewildered look, the waiter returned the wine to the kitchen and came back with a bottle of water. "Water isn't included in the meal," he patiently explained. "The cost will be put on your bill."

We had never seen bottled water before and thought it absurd that we should have to pay for it. "No, we don't want bottled water," Gordon insisted. "We want glasses of water from the kitchen."

Again the baffled waiter wandered off, bottled water in hand. Finally, he brought us each a glass of lukewarm water (no ice). The next day our stomachs informed us that it would have been wiser to pay for the bottled water.

Maryel Moyer, a longtime missionary, shares her experience with water. "Shortly after we arrived in Acornhoek, South Africa, in 1972, our water was declared unfit for human consumption. Even before that announcement, missionaries boiled their drinking water. We had a 10-gallon electric urn that sat on the kitchen counter, and mornings I made certain that our drinking water went through a 20-minute rolling boil. All of the mission station's water faucets were removed so that thirsty children would not be tempted to drink unsafe water."

When Gordon and I are traveling, if we are not sure of the local water, we drink bottled water or canned soft drinks. And we do not ask for ice cubes in our glasses. Also, we don't eat raw vegetables in places where they may have been washed in contaminated water. The first time we visit a country, we ask specific questions about water. The citizens will always know clean sources of drinking water.

When in our own home, we learned to keep a supply of drinking and cooking water in large containers. Some people add chemicals, usually purchased in tablet form, to purify their drinking water. If fuel is available, some boil water for 20 minutes to purify it. Note that the higher the altitude, the longer it takes for water to reach a boiling point.

In the two Middle East countries where we lived, water was rationed. It was only pumped to our area of town for 24 hours once a week. Life flowed around the arrival of city water. Cleaning the house, washing the clothes and the car—even baths—were scheduled to happen during that important day. Water flowed into galvanized-steel, two-meter (six-

Rooftop water tank in Jordan

19

foot) tanks sitting on the flat roof of our apartment building. On water day we could use the water without depleting our stored supply.

It was important to pay attention to the three faucets above the kitchen sink. The two regular faucets for hot and cold water received their supply from the storage tanks. The third, a single faucet set apart from the other two, was hooked into the city water system. Water only flowed from this faucet when city water was turned on in our area. We learned to never drink water from the storage tank— that is, unless we wanted stomach problems, as mosquitoes, water spiders, and bacteria thrived in sun-heated, rooftop containers. Once installed, the water tanks were rarely emptied and cleaned.

In Amman, if we miscalculated and ran out of tank water, Gordon drove out of town to a freshwater well and ordered a truck of water from one of the waiting drivers. This expensive method took lots of time, and delivery might not be the day of the order. Going up on the roof to check our water supply before doing laundry or taking baths became a part of our regular routine.

Helpful information for world travelers

United States	British Commonwealth
1. Fahrenheit (F.) scale used to measure temperature	1. Celsius (C.) scale used to measure temperature
2. Water freezes at 32 degrees F.	2. Water freezes at 0 degrees C.

3. Normal body temperature is 98.6 degrees F.	3. Normal body temperature is 37 degrees C.

An item missing in all of our overseas homes was a water heater with its own thermostat. It never occurred to us to ask about heat and hot water when we moved into our first apartment. After all, when we rented the place, we could see that each room had a radiator. And the kitchen and bathrooms had hot and cold water faucets. Only after we signed the rental contract and settled in did we realize that the landlord controlled the heat and hot water. Nor did we know that rental laws stated hot water would only be available during specific hours—usually two hours in the morning and evening. Since it took more than two hours for the water to heat, we really never had hot water.

Washing diapers for our three babies became a huge chore. (We didn't have disposable diapers in those days.) We bought a washing machine that had a heating cycle. It took an hour for the water to become hot enough to wash a load of diapers. By the time I added the washing cycle plus the time needed for heating the rinse water, I was lucky to get two loads of wash done by lunch! The washing machine literally ran the whole day that city water was available.

Unfortunately for us, the heat for the apartment was also controlled by the landlord and regulated by law. Turning the heat on didn't depend on the temperature outdoors; it depended on the calendar date, as the contract stated that the heating system would function from November 1st to March 31st. It didn't matter if a fierce rainstorm struck in October or that April could be damp and cold. The law was the law. We finally moved when we found an apartment where the renter (us) controlled the heat and hot-water system.

Upon moving to Papua New Guinea, we were introduced to a water system controlled by nature. Our home had a huge, round storage tank in the backyard. When it rained, the runoff from the metal roof was directed by gutters and pipes into the tank. With a rainfall of 250 inches (6.25 meters) a year, we rarely ran out of water. But in a long, dry spell, such as a week without rain, Gordon would pound on the tank to find the water level, and then I would make decisions about mopping and washing clothes. (The pounding on the tank would echo once the hit on the tank was above the waterline.) We did have to pump water from the ground tank to a small solar-heating system tank on the roof. How easy it was to forget the pump was on, only to be reminded by the sound of water cascading off the roof.

According to retired missionaries Grace and Henry (better known as Harry) Stevenson the water situation in Bolivia was much like that of the Middle East. The city of La Paz piped water to the buildings of the Bible institute, and it was OK to use this water for washing, cleaning, and bathing. But it was not safe to drink. The Bible school's flatbed truck would be loaded with barrels and driven to a fresh-water spring. Then full barrels were distributed among the campus buildings. The drinking water was carefully doled out to thirsty children and adults alike.

One furlough in Ireland, the three Stevenson children were outside playing games. After a while they became thirsty and asked their granny for a drink. She just opened the tap and gave each one a full glass of water. When they finished, she offered them a refill. "Can you really spare it, Granny?" they asked.

Helpful vocabulary

United States	British Commonwealth
1. bathroom, rest room, ladies' or men's room, the john, the head	1. toilet, loo, lavatory, WC (water closet), powder room, the ab (ablutions block—Australia)
2. outhouse	2. dunny (Australia)
3. faucet	3. tap
4. trash, garbage	4. rubbish
5. trash can, garbage can	5. rubbish bin
6. bathroom sink	6. basin

A sensitive subject needs to be discussed in this section on water—toilet flushing. Our family of six soon realized our water supply was not adequate enough to flush after every visit to the bathroom. We discovered the solution in a simple rhyme: "When it's yellow, let it mellow. When it's brown, flush it down."

But this ditty did not apply to the United

States! Retraining our children was required before our furlough times. We had to be explicit to meet the social expectations of our relatives and friends as well as fellow students and church members. "You must flush after every use, no matter the color," we instructed our kids firmly. I don't know if they ever understood why it was OK to waste water like that.

Another problem we faced involved toilet paper. Yes, we could buy it. But the slant of the sewer pipes in our homes didn't make it possible to flush it down the toilet. Trash cans with lids and lined with plastic bags were set discreetly next to the commode. Used toilet paper was thus discarded without clogging up the plumbing system. Of course, our children brought this disposal system back to the States. Unfortunately, most bathrooms did not have covered, plastic-lined trash cans with lids—an oversight that puzzled our children. But they soon found a solution. It took me a bit to realize that those small mounds of used toilet paper hiding in the bathroom corner indicated another retraining need.

Our first time overseas, we fully expected to use public toilets when shopping in town. You know, stop at the local gas station and use the facilities. Forget it! No usable public facilities existed in any of the countries we lived in. We learned to plan our route around the availability of toilets. Certain restaurants would let you use their facilities for the price of a cold drink, and certain grocery stores had facilities available to customers. Also some friends' homes were strategically located along the way.

Long trips away from any facilities demanded

creativity. In Papua New Guinea, with its jungles and plush gardens, we would stop the car and hunt for a "pathroom." Such spots simply did not exist in the Middle East. We learned to scan the dusty, bare landscape for herders and wandering flocks of sheep and herds of goats or camels or camping sites of Bedouin tents. When all we could see was telephone poles, we would pull over and open the front and back doors of the car. The place between offered some privacy. Our children had to be told this conduct was not culturally acceptable in the United States.

Throughout the world many people do not have access to city water—even one day a week. Bathing may take place in a river or lake, or not at all. Toilets may be built inside a shed with a hole that requires a squatting position. In island villages, small sheds may house seats built out over the water. In some places people wait until evening to find a private place.

When we returned to America after spending four years on the mission field, we never imagined that stateside water would upset our digestive systems. But it did. It seems that the new mix of natural minerals found in the water, plus the additives, such as fluoride and whatever chemicals were used for purification, would give us familiar stomach pains. Visitors from other lands may experience the same type of problems. Having bottled water available is a way to prevent difficulties. Whether traveling abroad or hosting visitors from overseas, it is always wise to have handy an over-the-counter medication for indigestion and diarrhea.

We became quite used to monitoring our water supply during the years we lived overseas. However, it never occurred to us that visitors to the United States might be concerned about the water shortage. We discovered that Papua New Guinea delegates to the 1985 General Assembly in Anaheim, California, found water shortages to be a worrisome issue. Right next to their hotel, a large plot of ground was planted in strawberries. Several days into the meetings, three of the delegates shared their concern with us. "We are all worried about the lack of rainfall here in Anaheim," they said. "Not a single drop has fallen since we arrived, and if it doesn't rain soon, those strawberries are going to die."

"It does not rain every day in Anaheim," Gordon quickly explained, "like it does in the highlands of Papua New Guinea. In fact, it probably will not rain in southern California for another four months." Gordon then explained that California does not have enough rainfall to meet the demands of the population, so water is purchased from other states and piped in to needy areas. He also told them about the process of irrigation—a method unheard of in the tropics. The delegates, fascinated with the whole idea of irrigating gardens, were delighted that the strawberries were not going to perish.

We know that, wherever we live, drinkable water is critical to survival. An important question everywhere will always be, "Should I drink the water?"

2 Should I **Eat** This?

"People don't eat things that aren't good."

I will never forget these wise words of veteran missionary Paul Orjala at our 1969 missionary orientation workshop. So, when we flew to Beirut, Lebanon, I fully intended to try every new food—and to like it! But I don't remember Dr. Orjala clueing us in to the fact that large supermarkets might not exist in our new destination. The truth is, grocery shopping—not sampling strange foods—produced mountains of stress.

In Beirut we did major shopping once a month, starting out early on Saturday morning with our list. We hit the fresh fruit and vegetable vendors' carts parked in front of several small grocery stores spread throughout the city before going inside. We soon stopped putting unattainable items on the lists, such as fresh milk products (we drank powdered milk), sour cream, mandarin oranges, and dill pickles, just to name a few. Within a few months I was using recipes that asked for locally available ingredients or using substitutes for impossible-to-buy items.

Stressful challenges were many: buying fresh produce using a new weight system, asking for and understanding the price in a new language, and using money with strange names (pound, piaster, peso, etc.) with different values than my home country's dollars and cents.

My first experience shopping in the open fruit and vegetable market in Beirut was unforgettable. In the States I was used to buying clean produce, often prepackaged in clear plastic and stamped with the weight and cost. In Lebanon carts heaped with produce lined the alley in the *balad*, the downtown area. Scales with weights sat balanced at the front of each cart with each vendor yelling his head off, trying to draw my attention to his wares.

Produce is sold by the kilo (2.2 pounds) in Beirut. During my first shopping forays, I had no idea how much a kilo of anything was. But I soon learned by counting individual pieces of fruit and vegetables, I would know when my choices weighed a kilo—about seven apples or tomatoes or tangerines. It was harder when the produce sizes were smaller. What complicated my shopping was that I didn't always want a kilo. Yet vendors became upset when I asked for a half-kilo of strawberries or green beans. Their mind-set was completely into selling by the kilo. I learned not to fight the system. Buying by the kilo and freezing the extra was much less stressful than insisting on less than a kilo of something. In the wonderful markets of Papua New Guinea, vendors stacked fruits and vegetables and set a price for each pile. I liked that.

Connie Patrick, a former Nazarene volunteer, remembers one of her first attempts to buy vegeta-

A Filipino feast—with lots of rice

bles in a street market in Albania. After choosing her purchases, she handed the vendor the money and asked, "OK?" He shook his head. She counted the money again. It seemed correct to her, but again he shook his head. After the fourth time, a crowd started gathering.

Finally another vendor came to Connie's rescue. "OK, OK!" he shouted. She gratefully grabbed her vegetables and quickly left. Later she learned that shaking the head from side-to-side meant "yes," and an up-and-down nod meant "no" in Albania.

In many countries clothes, household wares, souvenirs, etc., do not have set sales prices, especially in open markets. The merchants are out to make the biggest profit they can. When first asked, they usually quote an outrageous price. It is then up to the customer to bargain the shopkeeper down to a fair price. Thus, shopping becomes a game.

The merchants want to sell, and the customer—you—wants to buy. The game involves finding and purchasing what you want at your price, not theirs. Leave if you are feeling pressured into buying. Shopkeepers often become angry if you bargain them down to a fair price and then don't buy. The best advice is not to bargain unless you really intend to purchase.

Acceptable bargaining prices are set by the culture. In the Middle East, the shopper offers half the first price and then agrees to a price somewhere in the middle. Don't be discouraged when you try this. Think of a price you will be willing to pay, and then stick to it. If you walk out of the shop when the price seems stuck, the cost will come down if it isn't already at rock bottom. *The price is fair if you feel comfortable paying it.* If you enjoy your purchase, then consider it a fair deal.

Even a visit to another land's modern grocery stores with set prices can create cultural stress. Often the stock is stacked on shelves, but the organization of items varies greatly. For example, canned soup might be displayed beside the bleach. Usually, locally processed foods have labels only in the area's language. In languages with different alphabets, such as Arabic or Hebrew, pictures on labels help—although I once ended up with four cans of tomato juice instead of tomatoes. Even the English name for items may change, depending on the country of origin. Plus, free paper sacks for bagging groceries may not be supplied. I remember getting a cloth bag in Germany for my purchases. Germans know to bring their own bags to do their marketing.

Food and kitchen items

United States	British Commonwealth
1. Jell-O	1. jelly
2. jam or jelly (for toast)	2. jam
3. cookie	3. biscuit; slice (Australia)
4. biscuit	4. scone
5. napkin	5. serviette
6. dinner (large meal of the day)	6. dinner (midday meal)
7. tea (a hot drink)	7. tea (evening meal or drink with a snack)
8. supper (evening meal)	8. supper (light snack before bed)
9. sack lunch (brown bag it)	9. packed lunch
10. cookie sheet	10. biscuit tray or baking tray
11. teapot	11. kettle
12. special of the day (in a restaurant)	12. set menu (restaurant's special of the day)
13. flatware, stainless, silverware	13. cutlery
14. cutlery	14. knives
15. turner	15. fish slice
16. French fries	16. chips
17. potato chips	17. crisps
18. cream and sugar (served with coffee)	18. milk and sugar (served with tea)
19. pudding	19. custard
20. fruitcake	20. pudding

Another important tip is learning how to say "no" to aggressive, pushy peddlers who approach you on the street selling postcards, trinkets, and a wide assortment of items. If you are not interested in purchasing their wares, ignore them. Don't make eye contact. Don't smile. If you are pressed to buy, say a loud "no" and turn your back. Otherwise you might find yourself with a suitcase of unwanted merchandise. When shopping, you must be aware that pickpockets abound all over the world; therefore, guard your money and passport in public places. Gordon insists that the safest place for his wallet is a front pants pocket.

Much needed adjustment skills include using locally available ingredients and making substitutions in favorite recipes. Maryel Moyer explains what she did about milk in South Africa. "When we first arrived, I was told we could get fresh milk delivered once a week to the mission station. This sounded great, until I tried it a few times. I found many recipes for sour milk over the years. Later I bought powdered milk (we could actually buy the Carnation brand in those days). I quickly discovered that three months in a ship takes its toll on expiration dates; so immediately after purchasing powdered milk I mixed it in freezer containers. The day finally came when the grocery stores began stocking fresh milk. One time it was my turn to pick up milk at the town dairy. People on the station gave me their empty milk containers. On the way home one container leaked onto the carpet. Despite my scrubbing, that spoiled milk smell was hard to eliminate."

Then comes the process of adding new foods to the diet. Larry Buess, former missionary to Lebanon, shares his first response to new foods in Beirut. "I am shocked. Olives and yogurt are breakfast foods? You eat the leaves off grapevines? Bologna has pieces of olives and nuts in it? The flat bread we buy from glassed-in street carts looked like pizza. But manna-eesh (a pizza-like bread topped with olive oil and spices and then baked) delicious as it is, does not taste like pizza. Most people eat very little meat; it is used more as a flavoring than a main course. Butter is cheaper than margarine. At the butcher shop I point to a hanging beef or lamb carcass and say, 'Give me two kilos right off the back.' All beef cuts are the same price, meaning ground beef costs the

Cooking kebab on a traditional grill in Cyprus

same as filets. Going to the bakery every day for fresh bread is a must—warm, pocket pita bread, not sliced Wonder bread."

Diets change from country to country, but tasty food is found everywhere. Kitty Jones, retired missionary, writes: "In Kenya the staple food of cooked white cornmeal tastes bland, but rolling some into a little ball and dipping it into a bit of stew changes that. From Nairobi we moved 900 miles north to Addis Ababa, Ethiopia, where the food is very hot and spicy, and raw meat is a delicacy. We were delighted when our Ethiopian friends in Australia shared a hot, spicy meal of *injera* (baked pancakes) with us."

Vegetables all over the world are much the same, just prepared differently. The Bolivian staple is an Irish potato, but it is not boiled, mashed, or baked. Selected potatoes are dug up, spread on the ground, and frozen by the low night temperatures. After thawing in the sun, the potatoes are stomped with bare feet to remove the moisture. Done over a period of time, the potato shrinks to a remnant of its original size, and bags of potatoes are easily stored in a shed. When needed, the potato is soaked in water, and presto! you have *chuno*. This processed potato has its own unique taste, not recognizable at all as potato.

In many countries, uncooked produce grown on or in the ground must be washed in soap, iodine, or bleach before being eaten. Examples include lettuce, tomatoes, cucumbers, and radishes plus unpeeled fruit (strawberries, cherries, apricots, etc.). Shopping days require allotted times for washing fruits and vegetables before storing them.

Learning store hours saves us from wasting time. In Spain, shops open at 9 A.M., close from 1 to 5 P.M., and reopen from 5 to 11 P.M. In Papua New Guinea, towns shut down at 5 P.M., whereas in the Middle East major grocery stores are open 24 hours a day.

Every country has its set mealtimes; work and recreation revolve around them. These mealtimes might not match the schedule of your home country. During summertime in Spain, it is common to be invited over for a midnight meal and return home at 3 or 4 in the morning. A 7 A.M. breakfast the next morning is highly unlikely. The Arab world eats a light snack about 10 A.M., often in the office. A full lunch is served in the middle of the afternoon with light fare eaten later in the evening. Restaurants don't open for the evening meal until 7 P.M., with most diners arriving after 8. Adjusting to another land and culture involves not just menus but mealtimes as well.

Amounts of food vary from country to country. In Bolivia huge portions are served to guests; leftovers are taken home in bags brought specifically for that purpose. When attending a *mumu* in Papua New Guinea, where huge amounts of food are steam-cooked in a pit, the people also expect to take home leftovers. Guests in the Arab world know they are welcome by the overabundance of food offered at a meal.

In India, as well as other countries in the Far East, the people take off their shoes at the front door and sit cross-legged on a floor mat to eat. Food is picked up with the right hand only. Dessert, often fresh fruit, is served first. After the meal the hostess comes to each guest with a basin, bar of soap, jug of water, and a towel, and then washes her or his hand. Men are served first.

Sitting together over a cup of coffee or tea has strong cultural significance in many lands. In Brazil coffee is a celebration of relationships. During the day small cups of strong coffee are continuously served in homes and offices or bought at numerous coffee bars lining the streets. A cold drink, coffee, or tea is served to every visitor in a Middle Eastern home—a way of cementing relationships. Therefore, a drink should never be refused.

Enjoying a cup of Arabic coffee

"When I was in Haiti," shares Carolyn Parson Hannay, "people would walk for miles on dusty, sun-blistered roads to the mission station. After greeting them, politeness required that I offer a refreshing, cool drink of lemonade, limeade, or cola. If I didn't have these drinks, it wasn't acceptable for me to offer a drink that cost me nothing, such as water. I would say, 'Oh, Pastor, I am so sorry. I don't have any colas or orange juice or lemonade'—listing all the things I did not have and apologizing profusely. Then he would say, 'That's OK. Could I please have some cold water?' Only at his request could I serve him a 'free' drink."

In Haiti Carolyn always served her guests' drinks from a tray. "I needed to hold the tray with both hands," she explains, "and the guests served themselves. If no serving tray was available, a hostess could use a plate or even a disposable aluminum pie tin. In Haiti no one serves a meal on a table without a cloth of some sort, no matter how poor or humble the home. Most of the time a colorfully designed oil-cloth works as the covering."

When living in other lands, we don't expect our local guests to experience cultural stress. But they could. Jordanian Haidar Halasa really looked forward to his first meal in an American home. After the prayer, the hostess asked him, "Would you like some iced tea?"

The man had tasted iced tea and knew he didn't like it. So he asked, "What other drinks are there?"

"How about hot tea?" was the response.

Now Haidar was really in a pickle. Jordanians do not serve hot drinks with the meal—only after-

Pastor Haidar Halasa in traditional dress

ward. But he did not want to embarrass his hostess, so he accepted the tea. All during the meal, the cup of hot tea sat untouched. Only later did he learn that it would have been perfectly acceptable in an American home to request cold water.

The United States is the only country we have visited that has iced tea on restaurant menus and serves it as the drink of choice in their homes. Many non-Americans do not like its taste. In other cultures it is wise to offer a variety of drinks, from fruit juices to soft drinks to water to hot drinks.

When learning to survive in another culture, yearning for food from your home country is common. Dr. Donald Owens shares an experience he and his wife, Adeline, had in Korea. "After our arrival, Adeline and I lived in a Korean couple's home for our first six weeks. We had never heard the Korean language or eaten Korean food. Fortunately, the family spoke English quite well. As their guests, we ate only Korean food and soon experienced some of the trauma attached to cultural adjustments. We did not realize then that it was excellent food by any Korean standard. We just longed for a hamburger and a milkshake!

"I had $20 in U.S. currency and went to the U.S. Army post exchange (PX) to see if I could get in to buy something made in the good ole U.S.A.! The MP (military police) on duty said, "Sir, may I please see your pass or military identification card?" I had nothing like that, so I showed him my U.S. driver's license instead. "That's good enough for me!" he said with a smile. I bought cans of Campbell's soup, crackers, candy bars, and instant coffee. Adeline and I feasted until it was all gone but one Snickers candy bar. We measured that bar of candy to make sure it was evenly divided, laughing ourselves silly during the process."

Surviving in another culture will require many changes when it comes to food. Think of shopping as an adventure. Learn to eat locally available products. Master the money system. Enjoy new recipes and different tastes. Take advantage of every offer to eat safely prepared local foods. Remember, Paul Orjala had it right when he said, "People don't eat things that aren't good."

Bon appétit!

3 Do I Have the Right-of-Way?

Driving in a new country can be the most stressful and nerve-wracking adjustment of all. Take Beirut. It didn't seem like driving would be all that hard to us when we first arrived, as Lebanese drive on the right-hand side of the road, just like in the States.

Fellow missionary Larry Buess, soon after arriving in Beirut, described the traffic flow in a letter to his mother. "The thing that you notice most here is the way people drive. I have never seen anything like it. Drivers put one hand on the horn and the other on the steering wheel, propelling their vehicles toward their destinations without much regard to other traffic."

After arriving in Beirut, it didn't take long for the Buesses and Gordon and me to see that traffic patterns, based on a completely different set of traffic rules, controlled the drivers. Lane lines seemed to be painted for decoration only, as other drivers often ignored them and randomly chose where to line up at traffic signals. We finally realized that traffic in Beirut flowed like water—to the nearest empty spot! The width of the vehicles, not the white lines, determined how many lanes of traffic traveled down the road. All drivers appeared to approve of as many traffic lanes as a road could handle. Four lanes of cars on roads with lines painted for two was the usual pattern, especially during heavy traffic.

And those traffic circles! At least with stop signs and traffic signals we knew who was supposed to have the right-of-way. But traffic circles? It was every man for himself (and women too), and the vehicle that stuck its front fender into the circle first won. Needless to say, circles in Beirut were not places of quiet contemplation. Most drivers announced their arrival at a circle with a great deal of honking. Non-honkers were not taken seriously.

Tailgating was a fine art. In fact, if the prescribed U.S. distance between vehicles was allowed, that space was soon filled by three more cars. Speeds in Beirut were generally much slower then on a

A traffic circle in the Middle East

stateside highway, so driving somewhat closer than recommended by a driver's training course in the United States was possible.

An American friend in Beirut jokingly suggested that we should never look to the right or left when driving but keep our eyes on the road ahead. Then, if we were to be involved in an accident, it would not be our fault as we did not see the other car. Another friend suggested that we never use our rearview mirror. "You might have a heart attack," he quipped, "if you realized how close those vehicles following behind are to your precious piece of metal."

An Arab friend who had lived in the States gave us some important advice: "Observe and use the local driving patterns, as long as they don't put the safety of your vehicle or others in danger. If cars regularly turn left from the right-hand lane and vice versa, just watch your side and rearview mirror and be prepared to try it. Try to flow with the traffic wherever you are. You truly may be a danger to yourself and your passengers if you try to follow your own country's right-of-way rules."

Even though I learned to drive in heavy, southern California traffic, I was petrified to drive in Beirut. A year passed before I sat behind the wheel. And it wasn't just those driving patterns and the lack of road maps that put me off—it was that stick shift! (Only hot-rodders drove stick shifts where I came from. My father taught me to drive in his automatic-transmission Chevrolet.)

Perhaps if Beirut had been built on a flat plain, I might have been braver; however, our home was halfway up a mountain. I finally became weary of being tied to public transport or Gordon's schedule and accepted that learning to shift using a clutch was essential. I'm amazed that our Opal station wagon survived my grinding, lurching learning process. Just maneuvering our vehicle out of its tight parking spot between our apartment foundation pillars challenged me. I must confess that a few chips off those pillars can be attributed to my learning how to shift and drive at the same time. And I must admit that I was surprised at how much pleasure I got from gunning the engine and feeling the quick acceleration produced by a stick shift.

Helpful information

United States	British Commonwealth
1. drive on right-hand side of road	1. drive on left-hand side of road
2. steering wheel located in front of left front seat	2. steering wheel located in front of right front seat
3. stick shift on right of the driver's seat	3. stick shift on left of the driver's seat
4. gas (sold by the gallon)	4. petrol (sold by the liter)
5. self-service gas (pump your own gas)	5. full-service gas (pumped by an attendant)
6. trunk (car)	6. boot
7. hood (car)	7. bonnet
8. yield (to traffic)	8. give way (to traffic)

9. distance measured in miles	9. distance measured in kilometers
10. speedometer measured in miles	10. speedometer measured in kilometers
11. one mile = 1 1/4 kilometers	11. one kilometer (5/8 mile)
12. flat tire	12. puncture
13. cab	13. taxi
14. turn signals	14. indicators
15. motorcycle	15. motorbike
16. windshield wipers	16. windscreen wipers

Gordon learned to deal with diesel engines after we moved to Papua New Guinea. One experience stands above all the others. He was one of the missionaries who boarded the brand-new diesel bus of the Nazarene Bible College and headed for the coastal town of Madang for a men's retreat. The bus swept along like a dream over the potholed, dust-infested roads. Six streams had to be forded on the way to Madang. When the driver reached the first stream, he stopped, put the bus in first gear, and began to edge his way to the other side. Much to the dismay of the driver, halfway across the engine stopped, leaving the bus stuck in hip-deep water. All his efforts could not get the engine to turn over. Only one solution existed—the passengers took off their shoes, waded into the stream, and pushed the bus across the water.

The dripping wet passengers listened as the driver tried to start the bus again. No response. Dead.

"Check the battery cables," someone suggested. But the battery passed inspection.

Another man, who knew something about diesel engines, walked to the front of the bus and stooped to study the undercarriage. "Oh, no!" he exclaimed.

"What's wrong?" the rest of the men shouted in one voice.

"Normally, the air breather vent is on the top of the vehicle," he explained. "But the vent for this bus is located under the front bumper. So when we entered the stream, the engine sucked up water instead of air—and froze."

The damage was repairable, but the bus lacked a toolbox. The men stood stranded in the middle of nowhere. Miles of jungle surrounded them. They huddled together and prayed, "Lord, please send us help!"

After about 10 minutes, they heard the rattle of a pickup truck approaching in the distance. A government vehicle with a Filipino driver rounded the corner, splashed through the stream, and pulled up beside the bus.

"What's the trouble?" he asked.

"Our engine won't turn over."

"I'm a mechanic," he said. "Let me look."

The men told him about the placement of the air breather. He turned the key in the ignition. No response. "I agree with your evaluation of the problem," he said. "But not to worry." He went to his truck and took a spanner (wrench) from his toolbox and removed the fuel injectors from the engine.

After instructing the observers to stand back, he slid behind the wheel and turned the key again. Four streams of water immediately shot out of the engine about 10 feet up in the air. When the mechanic could see diesel fuel being sprayed, he turned off the engine, put the injectors back in, and bled the fuel line. The next time he tried the key, the engine started and purred like a contented cat. Accepting only thanks, the mechanic went on his way.

The missionary men praised the Lord for answered prayer and continued their journey. The approach to streams from then on followed a routine: the driver turned off the engine as soon as the tires touched water, and the soaked passengers pushed the bus across to dry land. From then on, Gordon checked the placement of the breather vent before attempting to drive vehicles through water.

Papua New Guinea presented us with a new set of driving rules, as cars drove on the opposite side of the road. We learned to compare right-side-of-the-road driving with left-side-of-the-road driving. All British Commonwealth countries—including Australia, New Zealand, India, South Africa, England, Scotland, Ireland, and Wales—drive on the left side of the road. And it irritates their citizens if someone insinuates that the left is the "wrong" side of the road. In a discussion about driving, it is wise to designate the difference as the "other" side of the road.

We found that being pedestrians could actually be more dangerous than driving when we visited countries that drove on the other side of the road, because, at first, we tended to look the wrong way for oncoming traffic. Americans automatically look to the left and then to the right before crossing a street, a habit that almost got us killed in our first visit to England.

Understanding speed limits in kilometers is a must in most places outside the United States. I once had a visitor to Papua New Guinea who sat white-faced and short of breath, his hands clinched in fists, all the way from the Mount Hagen airport to the hospital at Kudjip. As he scooted out of the car, he blurted, "Do you always drive 100 miles an hour?" He had not understood that my car's speedometer was in kilometers, not miles per hour. When the kilometer speed was adjusted, I was actually driving 65 miles an hour, the legal speed limit for the Highlands Highway.

Southern California, with its landscaped freeways, well-marked off-ramps, and carefully maintained surface roads, did not prepare me for driving overseas. I just presumed that local governments everywhere were capable of funding, building, and managing similar road systems. But the truth is that many countries on planet Earth cannot afford such complicated and expensive highways.

The words used for the various roads are often different from country to country—autobahn, freeway, divided highway, interstate, autostrada, concrete road, tarred road, turnpike, limited access, and so forth. For people traveling to another world area, the terms can be quite confusing. For example, the common word *interstate* in the United States is not used in other countries. Also, turnpikes or tollways in the

United States, which require a fee or *toll* to travel the road, are not common in many countries. While highways and freeways in the States usually have posted speed limits, many world areas do not place this restriction on drivers. For example, the autobahns of Germany, for the most part, have no speed limits. Also, the road condition or its type (paved, gravel, dirt, tarred, multilane, limited access, etc.) determines the speed a vehicle can travel.

Travel in Bolivia, as described by Harry Stevenson, echoes driving conditions in many parts of the world. "There were only six kilometers of paved road when we first arrived in La Paz. The rest were dirt. No signs lined the side of the road, warning of curves or needed road repairs. No speed signs regulated the flow of traffic. When I drove out of La Paz, I knew there would be few, if any, places to fill up with gas. I carried extra fuel on special racks built on my truck for five-gallon tanks. Sometimes fuel stored in barrels was available in a village along the way. To fill my tank, the fuel was pumped from a barrel into a jug and then added to my fuel tank via a funnel. The cost of this gas in a village was twice as much as in the city.

"Winding, single-lane mountain roads made for dangerous driving. Once in a while the road would widen just enough for traffic to pass. Uphill traffic had the right-of-way. In going up, if I saw a vehicle approaching me, I stopped at the nearest wide space. Downhill traffic was supposed to stop in the outside lane. But due to the lack of guardrails and huge drops into the valleys below, for safety's sake we stopped as far from the precipice as possible, being sure to leave enough room for oncoming traffic."

Efficient and cheap public transport is available in many of the world's big cities. Public buses are common as well as taxis that run a set route for a set price. In Bolivia these types of taxis are called *turfis*. In Beirut our family often took a *service* to crowded areas of the city that had no available public parking.

Gordon and I were surprised at the lack of American-made cars outside the States. We thought the whole world drove Fords and Chevrolets. But we found the Middle East full of Mercedes. The rich drive late models as a status symbol. Taxi and *service* drivers pay low prices for old model Mercedes that no longer meet Germany's tough road standards. Because they are so well made, they continue to run for years and years.

Papua New Guineans drive Japanese cars—Toyota, Mitsubishi, and Nissan dealers are in every major town. In the Middle East and Papua New Guinea, we discovered it was wise to buy a vehicle from a dealer that stocked spare parts and had trained mechanics. We personally never shipped a U.S.A. model car overseas because of parts and service issues.

Because we were residents, we always obtained a local driver's license when we moved to another country. We were granted licenses on the basis of our stateside licenses and were not required to pass a driving test; however, we had to pass a written test on international signs.

We know of countries where it is obligatory to

pass both a written and driving test. Drivers away from their home countries may not need a local driver's license for identification when stopped for breaking driving regulations. Many countries don't have the finances for traffic police or expensive radar equipment. But it is helpful to hold a license in the local language if you need to identify yourself at a roadblock or car registration check, or if you are involved in an accident.

Here are two important recommendations after more than three decades of driving in other countries:

1. Don't even think about driving in another land until you are sure your driver's license is recognized. Obtain an international driver's license, which must be obtained in your home country, and familiarize yourself with international road signs.

2. Be sure that you are covered by collision and liability insurance. In some countries only names listed on the car insurance policy are covered; therefore, visitors should not borrow vehicles. Insurance may be purchased with rental cars. Usually, your personal car insurance will not cover you in another land.

Newcomers should not immediately expect to feel comfortable when driving in another land. They should begin by first inquiring about the legal rules of the road. Being observant passengers, buying available maps of the area, and learning the landmarks for important intersection and areas of town are important keys to comfort. Driving with a passenger who knows the route the first few times and setting realistic time frames for arrivals at destinations also helps. Less anxiety rises, of course, when driving a registered, insured vehicle and holding a valid driver's license. Thus armed, the newcomer can throw away the panic button, recognize when he or she has the right-of-way, and even learn to enjoy driving in another land.

4 Should I
Kiss, Bow, or
Shake Hands?

After we attended our first Arabic church service in Beirut, the pastor asked us over for coffee. To our surprise, when we entered his home, all the guests stood up and shook our hands. I had already shaken everyone's hand when introduced after church just a few minutes earlier, so this practice seemed strange. Later when the first guest stood up to leave, everyone in the room again also stood and repeated the whole hand-shaking process.

In the culture of my home country, I basically shook hands when first introduced to someone or when I greeted them at church. In the Middle East, however, hand-shaking is much more a part of the culture. Friends and relatives expect handshakes or kisses, depending on the relationship, anywhere and every time they meet or leave. In many Asian countries people greet each other with a bow.

Friends of the same sex greet each other with a kiss in the Middle East. I had no difficulty kissing my women friends, but watching men kissing took some getting used to. Missionary Phil Rodebush says, "In the Arab culture, if I haven't seen a male friend in a while, the appropriate greeting was a kiss on the cheek. I did learn to appreciate and participate in this sign of friendship. My first Easter Sunday in Amman, Jordan, I worshiped in a large Nazarene church. Because Easter is a significant day for Christians, I was expected to greet all the men attending the service, even if I had just seen them on Saturday. The results of giving and receiving kisses from them were chapped cheeks from rubbing whiskers and lips worn out from puckering up."

Other cultures kiss for greetings as well. In Brazil married women kiss on both cheeks and single women get an extra kiss for good luck. The men shake hands when they meet, sometimes during their conversation, and when they part. Male friends freely give each other hugs—bear-type hugs. Touching each other on the shoulder and arms when conversing is common.

In Spain men greet men with a kiss on both cheeks or by touching cheek to cheek. In France a man may kiss a lady's hand.

Every aspect of public behavior is covered by each culture's own unique rules of etiquette. All cultures have defined, acceptable patterns of response to social situations. The first and easiest to observe consists of the rituals and words for saying "hello" and "good-bye." And this is just the beginning.

Learning correct social behavior began the day I arrived in a new country. The correct response to strangers, friends, and guests for all manner of occasions—births, graduations, engagements, funerals, church services, religious and national holidays—needed to be tailored to the new culture in which I lived and not to my own culture. I never learned of all of the subtleties and intricacies of the lands where I lived, but I did my best to learn what was expected of me culturally.

Hand gestures are a part of every culture. Some gestures are positive, such as the Brazilian thumbs-up sign for OK. Other gestures may be rude or even obscene. It is culturally significant to know which gestures are appropriate and acceptable.

Simple tasks like pushing an elevator button can cause stress. After living overseas for 33 years, choosing buttons in elevators still makes me ask, "What number should I push?" The right button is obvious when I am in my home country (United States), where the ground floor of a building is the first floor, the next floor up is the second floor, and so on.

In some countries the pattern of numbering a building's floors is different. The street level is the ground floor. On an elevator this floor may be marked with the numeral *0*, the letter *G*, or in hotels with an *L*. The next level up is the first floor, marked with the numeral *1*. In Jordan I lived on the fifth floor of an apartment building, but my apartment number was 4D and I poked the *4* button to reach my floor. As a result of this training, even today, if not careful to give it thought, I can end up leaving an elevator on the wrong floor.

Many countries follow traditional rites and rituals when it comes to engagements, weddings, and funerals. Among Christian families in Jordan, if the bride is not marrying someone within the extended family circle, the engagement is formalized by having men from the bride and groom's families meet together. Those present are asked if they have any objections to the union and other prospective grooms may be discussed. Once the men agree to the engagement, the woman is called into the room and asked, "Do you agree to marry this man?" If she answers "yes," the group drinks coffee together to cement the decision. An official engagement party will follow later in which the groom and relatives of both families present the bride with gold jewelry. The man and woman exchange wedding bands, which are worn on the right hand until the marriage ceremony is completed. Engagements are not taken lightly in the Middle East. Real commitment is expected.

Weddings can be as soon as a week after the formal engagement. The bride, wearing white, is accompanied by her extended family to the church. After the ceremony everyone shakes hands with the bride and groom and their relatives. No reception is held after the ceremony; instead a pre-wedding get-together is provided for family members the night before.

"In India marriages are arranged," explains missionary Norma Weis Morgan. "A couple meets for the first time at their engagement party the night before the wedding. In the West we marry the one we love. In the East they love the one they marry." Arranged marriages are common in many cultures.

Illness and death are surrounded with tradition and expected responses in every culture. If living in another culture and someone you know is ill or dies, you should ask about

An Orthodox wedding in Ukraine

- hospital or home visits
- times to visit the bereaved
- sending of flowers or money or delivering food items
- appropriate colors of clothing
- attendance at funerals and/or graveside services
- visiting the bereaved family during the year following a death

Other cultures have specific spoken phrases for these occasions, such as "I am sorry for your loss." Learning such expressions is vital.

Celebrating a child's first birthday with big parties is common in many countries because of high infant mortality rates for centuries. "In Bolivia," says Harry Stevenson, "two out of five children die from dysentery before the age of two. No social services, no employment benefits, no medical benefits, and extreme poverty explain this statistic. Christian parents dedicate a child before he or she dies; sometimes a small coffin is already outside on the bicycle."

Access to modern medicine produces higher survival rates, yet birthdays remain important cultural events. Koreans even celebrate a baby's 100-day birthday. Another big Korean celebration occurs on a person's 60th birthday, where her or his accomplishments are praised. Traditionally, retirement follows the 60th birthday, but in modern times the retirement age is 65.

Educational terms

United States	British Commonwealth
1. elementary school	1. primary school
2. high school	2. secondary school
3. 1st to 6th grades	3. 1st to 6th class
4. 7th to 12th grades	4. 1st to 6th form
5. university: freshman, sophomore, junior, senior	5. university: 1st to 4th years
6. major and minor (or emphasis on specific academic subjects)	6. "read" subjects (history, law, philosophy, etc.)
7. public schools (government funded and free)	7. national or government schools
8. private schools (school fees)	8. private or church schools (such as Eton)

"The East is very much a man's world," says Norma. "As you watch a Hindu couple walking down the road in India, you will note the wife walking nine feet behind her husband, thus giving him respect. She carries her baby on her hip, and to help her husband, she balances groceries or luggage on her head."

Missionary Harry Stevenson explains husband-wife relationships in Bolivian villages. "The man is the boss. He rides on the donkey; the wife and children walk behind. As she walks, she spins her wool. A woman is definitely the property of the man."

Some types of national holidays (such as Independence Day, Memorial Day, birthdays of important national leaders, and days that mark significant historical events) are shared by many countries. Some familiar and popular holidays in the United States and Canada (such as Valentine's Day and Thanksgiving) are not celebrated in all cultures.

Still all countries and cultural groups have national holidays that are peculiar to them alone. A few examples are:

1. *Chusok*—a fall holiday in Korea. Its date depends on the lunar calendar. Its purpose is to give thanks for the harvest and to visit the graves of the ancestors. Koreans who follow Confucianism take food and wine sacrifices to graves and bow to their ancestors. Christian families give thanks for the life of their ancestors during a special church service, either during Chusok or on the

anniversary of the death. All Koreans participate in big family gatherings—usually at the home of the eldest son—during this holiday.

2. Martyr's Day—on April 24. This holiday commemorates the 1915 massacre of Armenians in Turkey and is celebrated by Armenians around the world.

3. Santa Cruz Day—on November 12 in East Timor. This holiday, commemorating those who died in a government massacre following a political rally in 1991.

4. Doll Day or Girls' Festival—a spring holiday in Japan. Special food is served, and everyone wishes the girls health and beauty. At a girl's first Doll Day, her grandparents present her with *hina* dolls, which represent the emperor, empress, servants, musicians, and warriors of old. An elaborate and expensive display can be seven tiers high and hold up to 15 dolls plus miniature furniture.

5. Golden Week—a five-day spring holiday in Japan. Special celebrations include Green Day that celebrates nature and the environment; Constitution Day that commemorates when the 1947 post-World War II constitution went into effect; and Children's Day on which families wish their sons a good future. On Children's Day, the people hang carp windsocks (one per son) outside their homes and place samurai dolls inside, which symbolize strength, power, and success in life, as do the rice dumplings wrapped in bamboo leaves.

Living in another land necessitates embracing unfamiliar holidays. Not only will you share the joy and celebration with your new neighbors and friends, you will become a part of the community and country in which you live. That is a vital component of learning to survive in another culture.

"When Al and I moved from Nairobi, Kenya, to Addis Ababa, Ethiopia," Kitty Jones says, "we learned to make appointments using the Ethiopia Orthodox calendar. In addition to being 7 years back in time, the Orthodox calendar divides the year into 13 months. Christmas is celebrated about January 11 and New Year's in September. The Orthodox day begins at 1:00, which is about 6 hours different than the United States. When making an appointment, we had to clarify which calendar was being used as well as which clock setting, since 4:00 could also mean 10:00."

The world is divided into two distinctly different modes when it comes to time—clock-oriented or event-oriented. In a clock-oriented society, an occasion announced for 7:00 P.M. will begin at 7:00 P.M. In event-oriented cultures, starting times for occasions *are* announced, such as the wedding will be at 7:00 P.M. But that time is only a guideline for when people should arrive. The wedding will not begin until all expected guests arrive. It helps to understand which system is being used when keeping appointments or having guests in your own home.

In some places the system for mail delivery to individual houses and businesses does not exist. Instead, mail is received in a numbered post office box. And often mail delivery is not daily. It never took us long to figure out which days mail arrived in Lebanon, Jordan, and Papua New Guinea. We made mail runs on those days—without fail.

Becoming familiar with a country's sports teams is important. The rules and vocabulary of sports are absorbed into the culture, and stars become national —and sometimes international—heroes. Favorite sports become a part of the national personality; people are proud when their teams win.

Go to local sports events. If you have never played cricket and it is a popular sport where you are living or visiting, ask a fan to explain the rules. Football (soccer to most Americans) is the world's favorite

Ping pong is a favorite game in many countries

Playing soccer at an NYI camp in Lebanon

game. Kids in the poorest of countries can play on an empty lot or even in the street. People the world over will be glued to their television sets during the World Cup held every four years. Rugby League, Rugby Union, and Aussie Rules might, at first glance, resemble football in the States, but, in reality, they are much rougher, tougher games. Here is an Australian's advice about the United States game:

You should stop playing "American" football. The 2.5 percent of you who are aware that there is a world outside your borders may have noticed that no one else plays "American football." You should play proper football [soccer] instead. Initially, it would be best if you play with the girls, as it is a difficult game. Those of you brave enough will, in time, be allowed to play rugby, which is similar to American football, but does not involve stopping for rest every 20 seconds or wearing full Kevlar body armor like sissies.

Perhaps this negative assessment of American football—its suggestion that American athletes are wimps—shocked you. Accepting negative responses to your homeland, your government, your style of life, your religion is all a part of surviving in another culture. Appreciating the differences in lifestyle, in priorities, and in social values is a part of what makes living or visiting in another land so rich, so enjoyable. Prepare yourself for change, not just in habits and lifestyle, but also in mind-set. That is the secret for successfully adapting to another land and culture.

5 How Do I Say "Thank You"?

Learning a new language is by far the biggest challenge for persons intending to stay longer than a few weeks in another land. The more new residents understand what is being said in the local language the larger the comfort zone. Cramming doesn't work with language learning. The vocabulary plus every verb, every grammar rule, every sentence pattern needs to be mastered. Sometimes—as in Arabic, Russian, and Japanese—the new language has its own alphabet.

Babies spend a couple of years listening to and mimicking sounds before they speak in short, two- to three-word sentences that are meaningful. That same process (listening and mimicking) is also necessary when adults learn a new language—except it doesn't usually take as long, thankfully.

Learning a new language is easier if it is related to your mother tongue or first language. Take English and Spanish for example. Many English words are a derivative of Spanish words. In fact, some English words are spelled and pronounced nearly the same as Spanish, such as *capital* and *interval*. Derivatives make it easier to learn the vocabulary of some new languages.

When studying Arabic, I wasn't helped with derivatives, as few English words have an Arabic origin. Memorization and practice, practice, practice are the keys to language learning. And, yes, it is embarrassing for a 30-year-old to stumble and stammer through a three-word sentence. But a willingness to try plus an ability to laugh at mistakes are important keys to learning a different language.

After studying Arabic for 12 years, I thought learning Melanesian Pidgin English in Papua New Guinea would be a snap, because 90 percent of Pidgin vocabulary comes from English. Pidgin English is less complicated and has two grammatical rules I love. First, adding the word *ol* in front of a noun makes it plural. One woman is *meri*, but women is *ol meri*. Second, every verb becomes past tense by adding the word *bin* in front of it. Thus, "I go to school" translated into Pidgin is *Mi go long skul;* but "I went to school" is *Mi bin go long skul.* Pidgin, like all languages, has a grammatical structure that needs to be followed to communicate well.

One common mistake of language learners is to literally translate phrases from their mother tongue into the new language. Early on Phil Rodebush made a habit of translating the typical American greeting "How is everything?" into Arabic *Kiif kull ishi?* It was not long before he realized that Arabs would never use that phrase.

"American culture wants to sum up everything in a couple of sentences," Phil says. "Arabs typically ask individual questions: How are you? How is your job? your family? your parents? How is your ministry? Unfortunately, I did not discover this until I had already used the phrase *Kiif kull ishi?* so much that both pastors and youth laughingly greeted me with it my first two years in Jordan."

In his studies Phil learned the Arabic phrases for special occasions. One night he came in late from being with a group of friends and noticed a gathering at his neighbors' house, to which he was immediately invited. "I was exhausted and really didn't feel like joining the group," Phil says, "but I thought it would be a good idea to get to know them better. I believed it was a party—until their somber faces finally registered. One of the young men told me that his father had just died. My tired mind was trying to remember what to say when someone had died. I had already decided that I would convert whatever I said into the plural form—which I was quite proud of just learning—and thus share my words of comfort not just with my friend but also his whole family. I guess my mind had organized weddings and funerals in the same category and filed them under 'special occasions.' Before I knew it, I said, 'The same to all of you' in the plural form to a room of about 20 family members. To my chagrin, that is the way to greet single men at a wedding! Talk about being embarrassed!"

Larry Buess tells about using Arabic when asking a pastor for help. "While in Beirut we lived in an apartment in our Ashrafiyya school/church building. Years before we arrived, missionary Don Reed had planted grapes. I'm sure that Don had faithfully cared for the vines, but a few years had lapsed, and

How can you talk without using your hands?

they really needed to be pruned. I had no grapevine pruning experience.

"One of our Armenian pastors had been a farmer, so one day I asked him, 'Bogos, will you show me how to prune the grapes?' The Arabic word for grapes is *annab* and for rabbit, *arnab*. I used the wrong word in making my request. With a puzzled look on his face, Pastor Bogos said that he would help me. When we reached the grape arbor, he began to laugh. 'I thought you brought me here to skin a rabbit,' he said. I think he was relieved to only prune grapevines."

Dr. Donald Owens shares this story. "After studying the language in Korea for a year, I was asked to perform a wedding for the daughter of our district superintendent there. I had the ceremony translated from the Church of the Nazarene *Manual* and practiced the Korean language text over and over, trying to get it perfect. Korean is a phonetic language and each sound must be exactly enunciated.

"On her wedding day the bride walked down the aisle with a downcast face. No smile. No expression of joy. I thought this strange behavior for a beautiful and happy bride. However, I later learned that an old Korean custom demanded that the bride not smile on her wedding day, because if she smiles or laughs their first child will be a girl. The culture preferred sons, as they were the 'retirement plan' in a country that then had no work- or government-related retirement benefits.

"During the wedding I said, 'Now, I will ask the *shin boo* (bride) some questions.' But what I really said was 'Now, I will ask the *shin moon* (newspaper)

Learning another language

68

some questions.' The bride burst out laughing. This meant I would be blamed if their first child were a girl. Happily for me, they had a son first, so there may not be anything to that custom. However, on our next anniversary when my wife, Adeline, and I looked at our wedding pictures, we noted that she wore a big smile. We have four daughters!"

Ivan and Virginia Lathrop arrived in Amman, Jordan, to be missionaries without knowing one word of Arabic. "Finally, we found a good teacher," Ivan said. "She was lavish in her praise, and I was sure that I was her best student. One day Virginia did exceptionally well in her lessons, and the teacher was so pleased she planted a big kiss on Virginia's cheek. I then decided to forget about doing exceptionally well if it resulted in that kind of response.

"Virginia worked hard on her market vocabulary, but mistakes were to be expected. She once asked for a kilo of *hammar* (donkeys) instead of *hammod* (lemons). This was nothing compared to my error with the same word," Ivan admitted. "Our teacher asked me the basis of the Moslem calendar. I responded with *hammar* (donkey) instead of the *Qammar* (moon). She urged me never to make that mistake again as I might not be given either the time or opportunity to explain."

Language learning becomes even more confusing when trying to learn a third language. Connie and Bill Patrick, Nazarene mission volunteers, first served in Albania, where Albanian was the primary language. Later they worked at European Nazarene College in Switzerland, where the people spoke Swiss

German. "Imagine our surprise," says Connie, "to find that the Albanian word for 'no' (*jo*, pronounced yoh) was very similar to the Swiss German word for 'yes' (*ja*, pronounced yah). Albanians shake their head sideways for yes and nod their heads forward, chin down, for no. Visitors to Albania are constantly confused, and the Albanians find us strange indeed."

Miscommunication often happens between English speakers from different countries. Karen, a missionary from Australia, joined her new team members for the first time. At the beginning of the session, the leader suggested, "Let's break the ice by sharing our favorite holiday."

Karen quickly began to think of all the places she went on holiday, like the beach or the mountains. Much to her amazement, the Americans began to talk about specific days, such as Christmas and Valentine's Day. This was her introduction to the difference in the meaning of the word *holiday* as used in the United States. A holiday in Australia would be the same as an American *vacation*—a length of time away from work. Christmas and Easter are thought of as religious celebrations, not holidays.

Vocabulary

United States	British Commonwealth
1. smart	1. brilliant
2. delicious	2. gorgeous
3. steal	3. nick
4. cheat	4. crib
5. line up	5. queue

6. shut the door	6. pull the door closed
7. vacation (usually more than one day)	7. holiday (more than one day)
8. stores (places to shop)	8. shops (places to shop)
9. pack away (something in a box)	9. store
10. elevator	10. lift
11. pill	11. tablet
12. mail	12. post
13. Kleenex	13. tissue
14. hotel room with a private bath	14. en suite
15. vacuum cleaner	15. hoover
16. bangs	16. fringe (bangs has a sexual connotation)
17. comfortable dress	17. homely dress
18. hold the baby	18. nurse the baby
19. nurse (to breast-feed a baby)	19. breast-feed
20. yarn (for knitting)	20. wool (for knitting)
21. flashlight	21. torch
22. wrench	22. spanner
23. clothes rack	23. clothes horse

Before I traveled overseas the first time, I realized that speakers of English from other countries had a different accent. But I certainly expected to understand all that was said by English-speaking people. That did not happen. The first time we watched a British TV program, it seemed the actors spoke in a "foreign" language. Many idioms, terms, and cultural references flew right over my head. Learning new meanings for familiar English words is a must for English speakers traveling outside of their home countries.

Clothes vocabulary

United States	British Commonwealth
1. sweater (buttons down the front)	1. cardigan or jumper
2. dress	2. frock
3. jumper (sleeveless dress)	3. pinafore
4. swimming suit or swimming trunks	4. swimming togs
5. undershirt	5. vest
6. shorts/briefs/ underwear (male)	6. underpants
7. panties (female)	7. knickers
8. vest	8. waistcoat
9. windbreaker	9. anorak
10. sports jacket (with brass buttons)	10. blazer
11. slacks/pants	11. trousers
12. half slip	12. underskirt
13. baseball cap	13. sun hat
14. nightgown	14. nightie
15. tennis shoes	15. runners
16. panty hose	16. tights
17. suspenders	17. braces
18. diaper	18. nappy
19. clothespins	19. pegs
20. wool (type of fabric)	20. woolen (type of fabric)

While on furlough, a European missionary couple held deputation services in the United States. After several services in Arizona, they began the long, steep drive up the mountains from Phoenix to Colorado. As the road became steeper, they observed occasional signs that read "Turn Off AC." They didn't understand the signs' meaning, so kept right on going with their air-conditioner on full blast in the 100-degree F. heat.

Close to the mountaintop, the car engine began to sputter and then abruptly died. Since they had an AAA (American Automobile Association) membership, they were able to call for a tow truck. When the driver from AAA finally reached them, he was quite upset. "Didn't you see the signs telling you to turn off the AC?"

It was never hot enough in their home country to need air-conditioning in their cars. And even if they did have air-conditioning, it would not have been called AC. This was a painful way to learn the meaning of those two little letters in that context.

Dwellings and furnishings vocabulary

United States	British Commonwealth
1. ranch; ground-level house, one floor	1. bungalow or detached
2. duplex	2. semi-detached
3. apartment	3. flat
4. townhouse	4. terraced house
5. public or government housing	5. cooperative or council housing

6. condominium	6. apartment
7. mobile home (type of house)	7. mobile home (rented for a holiday)
8. subdivision	8. estate
9. front door	9. hall door
10. sliding-glass door	10. French door
11. yard (grassed area)	11. garden (grassed area)
12. garden (for growing vegetables)	12. vegetable garden/plot
13. paved area	13. yard; paved area in back of house
14. living room	14. sitting room
15. den	15. family room
16. baby crib	16. baby cot
17. twin bed	17. single bed
18. comforter	18. eiderdown; duvet
19. stove	19. cooker
20. oven rack	20. oven rails
21. decorator pillow	21. cushion
22. for rent	22. to let
23. real estate agent	23. estate agent
24. open/close the curtains	24. draw the drapes

A British missionary couple visited the States for the first time to hold deputation services. In making conversation in a person's home, the wife asked, "How do you like your garden?" The answer was "We're not into gardening." The visitor from England was confused, as she could see grass in the front and back of the house. It took awhile before she realized Americans call those grassy areas *yards*, not *gardens*.

Mistakes are bound to happen when learning another language. Below are a few examples where words are similar and easily confused. Imagine the embarrassment or humor created by the following:

- Italian—(Martin) Luther and uterus; horses and cauliflower; children and beans; woman and a great big woman
- East Timor—eggs and men
- Arabic—dog and heart
- Portuguese—pliers and steak
- Japanese—ticket and stamp

Mary Mercer, former missionary in Korea, shares her most embarrassing language learning gaffe. "Tim and I were in the second year of study at the university in Taejon, South Korea. One of our teachers was a gracious, humble Christian man. One day he came to class wearing a new suit. In my limited Korean I tried to say, 'Oh, Professor, you have bought new clothes.' But what I actually said was, 'Oh, Professor, you have bought new underclothes.'

"I immediately realized my mistake and proceeded to look for a hole to crawl in. The clincher was that the teacher had bought new underclothes and was wearing them too. Unknown to me at that time, Koreans take a casual view toward underclothes—everyone wears them, after all. So he simply parted a space between the buttons on his dress shirt and replied, 'How did you know?' So went the day in the agony of learning another language."

Translating from one language to another can be

quite tricky. While Betty Sedat was involved in Pokomchí translation of the New Testament, she very reluctantly left her five local assistants with a week of assigned work and went to western Guatemala for a missionary retreat. The helpers each took verses from the Gospel of John and roughly translated them on 3" x 5" cards. These were then passed around the worktable for the others' input.

After Betty's return, she showed fellow missionary Harold Ray the stack of cards completed during her absence. One verse talked about Jesus as the Lamb of God. Since no sheep live in that mountain region, no word existed for lamb in the local dialect. The helpers suggested calling Christ the "Goat of God," using a local word. "Jerusalem horse" was the translation for camel. Figs and olives became "peaches and avocados." And since tortillas are a sta-

Cell phones, used for communication everywhere, are popular with Lebanese

ple food of the Pokomchí, the Bread of Life was translated "Tortilla of Life."

The Wycliffe coordinator who reviewed the words said, "The tortillas can stay, but the peaches and avocados have to go!" For "lamb" they were forced to use the Spanish word *cordero*, as well as the Spanish word for "camel." These changes were against the wishes of the Pokomchí brethren, who wanted a pure Mayan New Testament that used no foreign words.

Methods for learning another language vary among Nazarene missionaries. Some attend schools established specifically for religious workers, while others attend national universities or obtain tutors. Whatever the method, the need to communicate in the language of the people is paramount to finding both comfort and success while surviving in another culture.

6 Is Worship on Friday, Saturday, or Sunday?

Christians traveling to another land may experience, for the first time, a culture whose very fabric is woven with tradition and day-to-day routines built around a non-Christian faith. Surviving in another culture, especially for evangelicals, often demands becoming familiar with the tenets of a new faith. In addition, blending into the culture enough to be approachable and to approach others with the Good News is a must.

Even countries called "Christian" include citizens who practice a non-Christian religion; yet the culture of Christianity predominates the society. For example, schools all take a Christmas break, and Easter is a time for families to be together, for new spring clothes, for celebration.

The truth is that every country has holidays built around its religious beliefs. Governments choose official days off work around the majority religion of the population; therefore, weekends are not always defined as Saturday and Sunday. For example, Friday is the day for noon prayers in Islam. So in a country like Jordan the government weekend is Friday and Saturday. Christian schools and institutions in Jordan close on Friday and Saturday. Sunday nights are the most heavily attended worship services, because the government-set weekend controls work schedules.

Christians do worship on Fridays in some Muslim countries. In Israel, Jews begin their worship day on Friday evening and finish on Saturday evening. The three major monotheistic religions worship side-by-side in Israel. Shoppers adapt to Muslim stores closing on Friday, Jewish stores on Saturday, and Christian stores on Sunday.

The attitude toward time definitely carries over into everyday life, including worship. In Papua New Guinea the Sunday morning service may be announced for 10 A.M., but nothing happens until the regular attendees arrive. Missionary Harry Stevenson says that Bolivians in the altiplano (high plains in the Andes Mountains) follow this same pattern. "Villagers ride donkeys or walk a long way to worship, and the Sunday meeting is the event of the day. A one-hour service would not be worth the effort. A two-hour block would be the minimum,

An evangelistic street service in the Philippines

Mawia playing an Arab musical instrument called an *aoud*

filled with singing, testifying, praying, and preaching. Often the whole congregation prays aloud at the same time. The Holy Spirit is given complete freedom to move among the people with no time restrictions.

"In the rural areas of Bolivia sermons are usually translated from Spanish to either the Aymara or Quechua languages," Stevenson says. "In the case of a visiting English preacher, the message requires double translation. Congregations are patient, and God works even with this unwieldy approach to proclaiming His Word. The people have no urge to hurry home; their minds and spirits are completely focused on worship."

Although the Church of the Nazarene has work in 150 countries (as of February 2006), it is not the dominant church or majority denomination in any of them. This means that Nazarenes ministering in other lands face a huge range of religious beliefs and practices, many of which are completely unheard of in their home countries. And in some countries it is illegal to try and convert citizens of the majority religion.

What is the key to reaching the world for Christ? *Respect.* Respect for the lifestyle, the culture, the language of the people. Respect for their religious beliefs and observances—many that require tremendous effort and sacrifice to please their god or gods.

We must respect their desire to experience some reaction, some sign of approval, some acknowledgment from their god or gods. This includes animists who worship the spirits of all living things as well as the spirits of their dead ancestors. This includes the Hindus with their myriad gods. This includes Muslims and their desire to please God through rituals and good deeds. It even means respecting those who deny the reality of God. Unless we respect people as we find them, we will never be able to cross the bridge to witnessing to them about God's wonderful gift of His Son, about the forgiveness of sin, about becoming a part of God's family.

It is risky to travel to another land, to weather the countless adjustments necessary to make it feel like home. But the fulfilling of the Great Commission demands that we all do our part. Whether traveling to another land for a short-term, cross-cultural mission or answering the call of God to serve a lifetime as a missionary, you can, by God's help, survive in another culture.

Call to Action

What about you? If God has not called you to be a missionary, are you exempt from "missionary-type" responsibilities? Definitely not! Missions needs you to be a passionate, committed supporter. Author Pat Stockett Johnston suggests the following ways to support missions:

1. **Pray** for the LINKS missionary family assigned to your local church. After reading *Should I Kiss or Shake Hands?* you understand that surviving in another culture demands a multitude of adjustments. Pray for God's love to reach out through your LINKS family's ministry in the culture where they live.

2. **Pray** for God to reveal to you what He wants you to do, for you can be sure He wants you to be involved in missions by being sent or supporting the sent ones.

3. **Prepare** children, youth, and adults, through the church's mission education program (NMI), to serve God, explaining His special call to missionary service and giving opportunities to respond to that call.

4. **Provide** for those the church sends by giving to the World Evangelism Fund through faith promise events, to Easter and Thanksgiving Offerings, and to special offerings, such as Alabaster, World Mission Broadcast, and Nazarene Compassionate Ministries.

5. **Participate** in a cross-cultural ministry at home. Opportunities include teaching ESL (English as a second language) classes, helping at a rescue mission or compassionate ministry center, becoming a Good Samaritan church, and helping with other missions projects.
6. **Participate** in a cross-cultural ministry in another land. Opportunities include Work & Witness, Mission Corps, Youth in Mission, and other special projects.

You may send an E-mail of encouragement to the author, Pat Stockett Johnston, and her husband, Gordon, at <WriterPat@charter.net> or by writing to them at 6384 Oak Ave., Temple City, CA 91780. Check out Pat's Web site at <www.patstockettjohn ston.com>.

Wes Eby, editor

Pronunciation Guide

The following information will assist in pronouncing some unfamiliar words in this book. The suggested pronunciations, though not always precise, are close approximations of the way the terms are pronounced.

Acornhoek	AY-kohrn-hook
Amman	ah-MAHN
annab	AN-nuhb
anorak	AN-uh-rak
arnab	AHR-nuhb
Ashrafiyya	ASH-rah-FEE-yah
Aymara	ie-MAH-rah
balad	BAL-uhd
Beirut	bay-ROOT
Bogos	buh-GOHS
bon appétit	boh nah-pay-tee
bureau de change	BYOOR-oh duh CHAYNJ
chuno	CHOO-noh
Chusok	CHOO-sahk
codero	koh-DAY-roh
en suite	ahn SWEET
Hagan	HAH-gun
Haidar Halasa	HIE-der HAL-luh-suh
hammar	HAHM-mahr
hammod	hahm-MOHD
hina	HEE-nuh
injera	in-JEH-ruh
Kiff kull ishi	KEEF KOOL LIH-shee

Kudjip	KOOD-jip
Madang	muh-DANG
manna-eesh	man-nuh-EESH
Mi bin go long skuol	mee behn goh long skool
mumu	MOO-moo
ol meri	ohl MEH-ree
piaster	pee-AS-ter
Pokomchí	poh-kohm-CHEE
Orjala	ohr-YAH-lah
Quammar	KAHM-marh
Quechua	KEH-choo-ah
service	ser-VEES
Taejon	TAY-JUHN
turfis	ter-FEES